THE BUSINESS TITHE

THE BUSINESS TITHE

A FAITH-BASED FRAMEWORK for PROFITABLE BUSINESSES THAT CHANGE THE WORLD

RICK K. JONES

Advantage | Books

Published by Advantage Books, Charleston, South Carolina.
An imprint of Advantage Media.

Printed in the United States of America.

10 9 8 7 6 5 4 3 2 1

ISBN: 979-8-89188-386-4 (Paperback)
ISBN: 979-8-89188-387-1 (eBook)

Library of Congress Control Number: 2026903027

Cover design by Lance Buckley.
Layout design by Megan Elger.

05-06-2026 9:19

This book is dedicated to the ministers, staff,
and good people of John Wesley United Methodist Church
in Charleston, South Carolina.
Our home church has been a joy for me and my family.

John Wesley once said,
"Do all the good you can,
by all the means you can, in all the ways you can,
in all the places you can, at all the times you can,
to all the people you can, as long as ever you can."
These are words to truly live by.

CONTENTS

ACKNOWLEDGMENTS

THERE ARE MANY people to thank for their contributions to this book.

First, thanks to my wife Charlotte, my daughter and fellow author Jennifer, and my son Ryan for their input.

Second, thanks to all the business leaders who influenced me and ran their companies the right way—with integrity, honesty, and an eagerness to give back to others. These include but are not limited to the late Homer Rice, the late Bob Cohn, Bob Vecchionne, Jim Host, Chuck Jarvie, the late Bill Battle, Gordon Whitener, the late Jerry Waters, Ron Cook, Devron Edwards, Marc Kidd, Jim Haney, Grant Teaff, Reggie Minton, Beth Bass, Steve Hatchell, Pete Derzis, Clint Overby, Nick Carparelli, the late Frank Craighill, Harlan Stone, Lisa Murray, the late Kristi Atkins, Mike Reisman, Bob Hope, Bob Heussner, Mike Hoffman, Mike Palisi, Steve Robinson, Kayleen Middleton, and Lindsay Collins.

Third, thanks to all my teammates and colleagues over the past forty-plus years who contributed so much to our successes and to the hundreds of clients and customers who entrusted their businesses to us.

Finally, thanks to my team at Advantage Media, including Adam Witty, Nicole Kupka, Ezra Byer, Shweta Ganesh Kumar, Whitney Rosenfeld, Olivia Tanksley, Heath Ellison, Shandi Thompson, and Lance Buckley.

ABOUT THE AUTHOR

RICK K. JONES is a veteran entrepreneur, marketing strategist, and author whose career spans more than four decades of helping brands connect with audiences through sports, entertainment, and lifestyle marketing. As the founder of agencies including The Strategic Group, The GEM Group, FishBait Marketing (now FishBait Solutions), and Heartland Pirates, Jones has built a legacy of profitable, purpose-driven business leadership. Jones also hosts the *Sh-Boom* podcast, specifically for the baby boomer generation.

In his latest book, *The Business Tithe: A Faith-Based Framework for Profitable Businesses That Change the World*, Jones challenges entrepreneurs to view generosity as a core business principle rather than an afterthought. Drawing from real-world experience, he shares a seven-step model designed to align profits with faith, purpose, and community impact.

Beyond his entrepreneurial success, Jones serves as captain and chief creative officer of Heartland Pirates, an organization devoted to reaching consumers who embrace traditional American values. He has contributed to America's 250th anniversary celebration through the United Tastes of America initiative, showcasing regional foods and heritage.

A fourth-generation Atlantan now living on Wadmalaw Island, South Carolina, Jones continues to write, speak, and consult on topics related to faith-driven entrepreneurship, purpose-based leadership, and stewardship in modern business.

And you will know the truth,
and the truth will make you free.

—JOHN 8:32

INTRODUCTION

"WE'RE AT A CROSSROADS in America." This is what I wrote in October of 2018, long before the coronavirus pandemic crisis, various natural disasters, and two contentious national elections. We are now seeing that we, as a country, have failed many of our constituencies and fellow citizens, and we seem to be mired in a sea of disillusionment.

Many of our problems feel unsolvable, and our government doesn't offer appropriate answers on either side of the aisle. Our political differences have made us less likely to engage with people with opposite views. Some of the *brutal truths* in American society today include the reality that businesses and the very foundation of capitalism are under attack.

More and more, business owners and entrepreneurs are being portrayed as selfish, greedy, and insensitive to the broader needs of society. The perception is growing that billionaires are becoming increasingly wealthy, while most others are falling further behind.

At the same time, a generation of young people is increasingly looking to institutions, particularly the government, for solutions to their personal struggles and broader social problems. Many Americans feel that the dream of upward mobility, of improving life for themselves and their families, is slipping out of reach. According to Pew Research, 47 percent of Americans believe the American dream is no longer possible.[1] They're convinced that the odds are stacked against them by forces outside their control.

Nature abhors a vacuum, and it is our responsibility to step in and help fill that void. I believe the time has come for small business owners to unite and show society the true benefits of capitalism. Together, we can push back against the drift toward socialism by leveraging our collective political, financial, and spiritual influence for the good of all.

History has shown that the extremes of socialism often lead to devastating consequences, restricting individual potential and creating artificial ceilings on success. As we can clearly see, the federal government, regardless of which party is in power, simply cannot and will not solve all of our problems.

At the same time, we must acknowledge that capitalism without a conscience can be just as harmful. When greed dominates, the culture suffers. We see it when senators use insider information to enrich themselves, when manufacturers inflate the price of lifesaving medical supplies, when insurance companies cancel policies in the wake of natural disasters, or when corporations use reduced taxes only to buy back shares instead of investing in employees or innovation. Capitalism rooted in selfishness undermines fairness, inclusion, and opportunities for all.

So, we the people need a new revolution to take back our country with values and principles for everyone.

---

1 Gabriel Borelli, "Americans Are Split over the State of the American Dream," Pew Research Center, July 2, 2024, https://www.pewresearch.org/short-reads/2024/07/02/americans-are-split-over-the-state-of-the-american-dream/.

What Are American Values?

We often hear the phrase *American values*. But just what does that mean? While our founding fathers were not perfect—after all, they left out many members of society then, including women, African American slaves and freedmen, and Native Americans—they sought to develop a society in which one could get ahead based solely on one's own personal initiative.

The American dream was available to all who sought to improve their lot in life, regardless of parentage, religion, nationality, or initial economic status. Men were free to pursue their personal dreams to provide for themselves and their families in any legal way they chose. Subsequent laws granted these same rights to women, African Americans, Native Americans, and immigrants who became American citizens, making our society one of expanded rights rather than increased restrictions.

I define the American dream as the ability to rise above any status you currently have to achieve whatever you want, if you work both hard and smart, regardless of age, sex, race, sexual orientation, or economic status. But in this crucial moment for our country, when so many Americans feel the American dream is for someone else and unattainable for them, we must do something. In many cases, sadly, they seem to be right. So we must do something to change both the narrative and the results.

How Do We Fix This?

So, how do we fix this? How do we come out of situations such as the coronavirus pandemic and natural disasters such as hurricanes,

I define the American dream as the ability to rise above any status you currently have to achieve whatever you want, if you work both hard and smart, regardless of age, sex, race, sexual orientation, or economic status.

tornadoes, and fires and prosper once again? How do we ensure that all Americans can and will prosper?

There's an old saying in athletics: If it's to be, it's up to me. It's time to apply that saying to the issues and ills of today's society, *one small business owner at a time*. And small business owners collectively, across this nation, can make a real impact. After all, there is nothing small about small businesses in America today. We saw this in full measure during the pandemic and recent disasters, as small businesses and their staff suffered greatly.

Let's start with my definition of a small business. I believe a small business is a privately held company that generates less than $4 million in annual revenue. There is no public stock trading or institutional investors, and it's a business in which you, the owner or owners, are in control of your own destiny and have the ability to shape the destinies of others.

"There are around 33.2 million small businesses in the United States."[2] They are the real economic drivers of our nation's economy. And most of these businesses generate less than $1 million in annual gross revenue.[3] Many small businesses today are owned by baby boomers. As these business owners look to retire by selling their businesses, closing their businesses, or passing their businesses along to others, there will be unique opportunities to leave a larger legacy.

This book is a simple process for setting the right priorities for your business, getting the most out of your business, and using your business as a vehicle to make a real difference in the world today. What follows are seven essential steps that each and all of us business owners

---

2 Gabrielle Carpenter, "Small Business Statistics in 2024," NAWBO Expert Reviews, March 6, 2024, https://nawbo.org/expert-reviews/blog/small-business-statistics/.

3 Mark Mayo, "Percentage of U.S. Businesses That Generate Under $1 Million Dollars," 601 Media, August 7, 2024, https://www.601media.com/percentage-of-us-businesses-that-generate-under-1-million-dollars/.

can take individually and collectively to rebuild the values and principles on which our country was founded and to make a real difference for our communities, our country, and the world in which we live.

My former company was called FishBait, a name that comes from the expression, "You have to fish or cut bait." That requires a bias for action, and I hope you, too, will start to act by joining me on this journey and implementing the seven steps of *The Business Tithe*. Together, we can change the world for the betterment of all.

In the Bible, Luke 12:48 says, "For everyone who has been given much, much will be required; and to whom they entrusted much, of him they will ask all the more." I hope you will join me in this movement to make the world a better place.

Rick K. Jones

Captain, Heartland Pirates

God created man in
His own image, in the image
of God He created him;
male and female, he created them.

—GENESIS 1:27

STEP ONE

VALUE YOUR WORK

DO YOU EVER wonder if what your business does actually *matters*? Does it really make a difference? Is all your hard work worth it?

The first step on the road to business, personal, and societal success is to fully realize, accept, and celebrate that work is not only good and important but is *divinely inspired*. The book of Genesis describes the creation of the world. No one really knows just how long it took God to create this world, but we do know that God is and was a worker.

The Bible says that God completed the world by creating man in God's own image. So, just as God worked to create the world in all its glory, he expects all of us to work to make the world even better than we found it. God showed his creativity in making the world, and he designed man to be creative as well.

Think how many wonderful things people have accomplished through their creative work down through the ages. Things such as ancient and modern cities, works of art, books, music and theatre, culinary masterpieces, and trips to the moon and back—not to mention creative breakthroughs in medicine, communications, and travel. Most of these things have been accomplished for the betterment of society.

Much has been made of God's commandment for us to work six days each week and to rest on the seventh day. We tend to focus on the "rest on the seventh day" part without thinking about those other six days of the week. Do the math. Six days is 86 percent of a week. Therefore, work is highly important to God and, more importantly, is *inspired* by God. Human beings are wired in their DNA to work and have been that way since the very beginning.

Humans wish to be productive and to accomplish goals. Our very survival depended on early humans working both individually and with others to find or grow food, create shelter, and protect themselves

Human beings are wired in their DNA to work and have been that way since the very beginning.

and others. And, for centuries, that is just what we have done. We have survived and we have prospered. Now that you realize that work is divinely inspired and really matters, you must also believe that your work is both noble and honorable.

First, you need to quit apologizing for owning a business or wanting to own or begin a new business that *creates value* for yourself and others. The private sector is essential to the success of a free society and to the overall success of our country and our world.

Business owners create businesses by investing and risking capital. Each of you has risked or will risk financial capital, along with countless hours and energy spent creating, developing, and nurturing your business without any guarantees that the business will be successful—because there are no guarantees for success. Owning a business is not for the meek or cowardly. That sound you hear at night while you lie in bed is your heart beating.

It takes guts, commitment, determination, effort, and resiliency. Yet, when done right, it also has incredible rewards. Think about how many associates, vendors, and customers your business has supported, not to mention the jobs you've provided for others. Your efforts have indeed been both noble and honorable, or they will be in the future.

Second, if you truly believe that work is noble and honorable, then you must do everything in your power to make sure you never betray this concept. This means you will not do anything unethical or immoral in running your business. If you do, we all suffer and are lumped in with those unethical businesses and businesspersons who fail to honor the nobility of business. Immoral and unethical businesses cause people to say that all businesses are bad. And that's just not true.

Third, we have a responsibility to make sure that those unethical and immoral businesses are identified, chastised, and punished as exceptions rather than the rule of all businesses. If those of us who run honorable businesses don't call out the cheaters, then who will? Is it fair that bad businesses and unethical businesspeople make it more difficult for the rest of us? No, but nobody ever said life was fair. Every time we fail to call out the bad guys, we get what we deserve.

Never confuse what is *legal* with what is *honorable*, because they are often very different. We know of lots of businesses that don't technically break laws but nevertheless fail to act honorably. One example is the now-defunct energy company Enron. Enron used *legally recognized* accounting principles that were nevertheless less than honest in their revenue projections. Each of their investors ultimately lost all their money. The glut of lawsuits polluting our legal system is yet another sign that people are failing to act in an honorable manner. We need to change that.

Finally, we have a duty to make our businesses the best they can be. We must ensure we are always working to help our businesses reach their potential because the more profitable our businesses become, the more people we can positively influence.

This leads us to step two.

Feed my sheep.

—JOHN 21:17

STEP TWO

FEED YOUR SHEEP

IN JESUS'S FINAL commandment on earth to Saint Peter, he implores Peter, not once but three times, to "feed my sheep." That means to serve people in every way. Businesses are not exempt from this concept. At their core, all businesses should exist to "feed sheep."

Is your business feeding sheep?

Think about a shepherd. Their job is to make sure the flock is safe and productive. It's the same for a business owner. Now, think about your flocks. That's right, you have more than one.

Your first flock is your family. At its core, your business exists to take care of you and your family. A successful business provides a family with not only the basics—such as sustenance, shelter, and security—but also, hopefully, prosperity. 1 Timothy 5:8 says, "But if anyone does not provide for his own, and especially for those of his household, He has denied the faith and is worse than an unbeliever."

I have seen so many small businesses that pay everyone except themselves, the business owner. That is a sin, because they and their families suffer. I understand and accept that business owners often need to make sacrifices in order to build a business, but these sacrifices should never impact their ability to live, pay their personal bills, and take care of themselves and their families. A business that fails to do this is not a healthy business. I build businesses first and foremost to feed my family. You should too.

Your second flock is your associates, those people who work side by side with you, as well as the families supported by your associates. Recently, there has been a lot of anguish and consternation over the federal government's Affordable Care Act, known more colloquially as Obamacare, and whether this administration is going to repeal or modify it. Now, I've read the United States Constitution, and I cannot find where it requires any business to pay for healthcare for its employees. That being said, I've always believed it was my moral responsibility to do just that.

I have sacrificed significant profits by funding 100 percent of my associates' health insurance, both individual and family coverage, because I thought it was simply the right thing to do, and I slept better at night knowing my people were protected.

Is your business doing all that it can for the people who work for it? The beauty of having a privately owned business is that, instead of placating shareholders, you can focus on taking care of stakeholders. There are no greater stakeholders than your associates. Think about how many families your business supports and how, in turn, those families then make contributions to their communities. That is real trickle-down economics, and it's what makes capitalism work.

It's relatively easy to take care of your associates when times are good. Our finest hour at FishBait Marketing was when the coronavirus pandemic shut down the sports and entertainment industry and we did not let anyone go. We found a way through a combination of governmental PPP support, a Small Business Administration loan, and a lot of personal funding to keep each and every one of our teammates gainfully employed as we waited out the pandemic. Conversely, we saw lots of people in our industry lose their jobs. Taking care of your associates is paramount to the success of your business.

Your third flock is your customers. Serving customers is the reason all businesses exist. Providing value to customers enables your business to survive and thrive. Every business should strive to do its very best in serving its customers, which includes charging a fair amount for the value of its product or service offered. Value occurs when both parties feel they have benefited equally.

Your fourth flock is the vendors and suppliers who sell you goods and services and that way enable your business to be successful. I

Taking care of your associates is paramount to the success of your business.

know many businesses that are slow to pay their suppliers. I believe this is wrong.

Most suppliers to small businesses are small businesses themselves, and cash flow is essential to their survival and growth. After all, they have flocks to feed too. Make it a practice to pay your suppliers in a timely manner. You'll find that they will treat you better and provide even greater service to you in return.

Your fifth flock is your church, synagogue, or mosque. I believe that God blesses businesses that bless and honor him. That means those individuals who contribute their time, talents, and money to further the mission of God here on earth. No church is perfect, but churches, synagogues, and mosques exist to collaboratively serve people and communities. Your business should support such activities.

Your sixth flock is your community. This includes those less fortunate than you in your own backyard. All businesses can find unique ways to support the communities they serve.

The best way I know to really determine a person's priorities is to look at their checkbook. How and where they spend their hard-earned money says a lot about a person and their values. I am often disappointed when a political figure releases their tax records, if they even do it at all, and I find they've given little or nothing at all to a church or charity. I find that to be the height of hypocrisy. It amazes me how certain politicians can give speeches day after day about wanting to serve their communities without actually personally giving anything to them. Like the old saying goes, put your money where your mouth is.

Successful business owners should serve the community where they operate. We often look outside our immediate area for causes to support, but the truth is that small businesses should focus on their local community. I'm not saying you shouldn't support charities doing good work in Africa and around the world, but you should also look to help in your own backyard. No matter how successful you think your community is, there is always some need nearby.

Your seventh flock is your country. I am unabashedly a very proud American. I truly believe that I live in the greatest country on earth and that its success is due to inherent American values that create ways for each of its citizens to succeed. Don't get me wrong, our country is not perfect. No country, organization, business, or human being ever is. But I've traveled extensively and even lived abroad for several years, and this country is still head and shoulders above anything else I've seen.

It's no wonder the rest of the world looks to America for leadership and assistance. I also speak with a lot of immigrants who have come to America for greater opportunities, and they are thankful for the opportunities they now have. That reassures me of the potential of America for all its people.

Speaking of the world, your final flock is the world at-large. A small business owner can create products, services, and funds to help others around the world. In many developing countries, a little can go a very long way.

My son Ryan and I recently traveled across the country, visiting all fifty states and recognizing and celebrating many of our nation's best restaurants as part of our *United Tastes of America* podcast series. Many of these businesses are multigenerational icons and beacons of their respective communities. We were impressed with so many of these places and the ways they have served their communities and continue to find ways to give back to their customers and communities. A lot of good things are happening out there, and a lot of sheep are being fed.

So, you now see that your business has both the potential and the mandate to feed a whole lot of sheep.

The one who had received the five talents came up and brought five more talents, saying, "Master, you entrusted five talents to me. See, I have gained five more talents."

—MATTHEW 25:20

STEP THREE

MAKE A PROFIT

AT SOME POINT and for some mysterious reason, the term *profit* became a negative one, despite the fact that only profitable businesses can feed sheep. Contrary to what some people believe, it is not a sin to make a profit. In fact, it's essential for our society or any free society to exist.

Only a profitable business can create and sustain jobs, and jobs are essential to maintaining communities. Only profitable businesses can consistently give back to their communities. Truett Cathy, the founder of Chick-fil-A, said it best when he summarized this belief with the statement, "No margins, no mission."

Chick-fil-A is a great example of a privately held business that serves its communities. It funds a camp in North Georgia, provides matching funds for college education to its young associates, donates *a large amount* of food to various organizations and events, and allows its owner-operators to participate in community work, among other initiatives.

Step three is to commit to being proud of owning a profitable business that helps many people. In steps four and five, we will show you ways to make sure your business is profitable, so it can provide for you and for others. But *this* is the place where I need to remind you that profits need to impact much more than just you personally. Capitalism without compassion is meaningless.

In the Gospel of Matthew, Jesus tells the story of a man who gives three of his slaves a set amount of money for both safekeeping and investment. The man decides how many talents he gives to each based on his perception of their abilities. Now, in Biblical times, a talent was a lot of money.

Most scholars believe it was roughly equivalent to the amount a common worker would receive for twenty years of work.[4] The slave who receives the largest amount, five talents, invests the money and doubles his return, achieving ten talents. The second slave, who receives two talents, also invests his money and doubles the return for his master. But the slave who receives only one talent, fearing he will lose the money, hides it away and creates no profit.

The master, upon his return, congratulates the two slaves who doubled his money but severely rebukes the slave who squandered his opportunity. By hoarding his money, that slave was operating from a mindset of fear and lack, rather than one of abundance, gratitude, and faith. Jesus shares this parable to illustrate that God wishes for all of us to take the gifts he entrusts to us and, with faith in our hearts, allow them to grow.

In other words, profit is not a sin. It is God's own intention.

So, how much profit should you aim for? Each business is different in how it calculates profit. Some have small profits per transaction but a large volume of transactions, which leads, aggregately, to large profits. Some have few transactions, so they need higher margins per transaction. There is no right or wrong answer here.

The various agencies I have owned sought to achieve a minimum of 20 percent profit after EBITDA (earnings before interest, tax, depreciation, and amortization). Profits allow you to do many things, including invest in your business with new products, services, and people. Profits allow you to provide bonuses to your team. And, yes, profits allow a fair return on investment for the business owner or owners.

---

4 "Fact: Talent," ESV.org, accessed September 16, 2025, https://www.esv.org/resources/esv-global-study-bible/facts-matthew-17/.

That being said, I believe that it is a sin for *all* of the profits of a business to go straight into the business owner's pocket. We'll explore that further in the final chapter. But the bottom line is that your bottom line *matters*. Profits allow your business to survive, grow, and prosper. And that's how you feed sheep!

I will instruct you and teach you in the way you should go; I will counsel you and watch over you.

—PSALM 32:8

STEP FOUR

EMBRACE THE PROCESS

ULTIMATELY, I BELIEVE that business success comes from what Coach Nick Saban, the ultra successful former head football coach at The University of Alabama, calls *The Process*. Steps four and five are both aimed at learning and mastering the necessary processes to ensure your business will become and remain successful and profitable. And get ready, because the process can be fairly lengthy and definitely tedious at times. After all, that's why we call it *work*!

Regardless of what your business makes, sells, or does, there are similar strategies that every business should use to succeed and flourish. We all know that the longest journey begins with a single step. The first step to improving your business is *your decision* to improve your business. Only you can take this critical first step. You must decide to change the way you feel, the way you think, and the way you work. Your attitude will determine your altitude. Remember, the person who says they can and the person who says they can't are both equally right.

Change is hard. Human beings hate change. But if it were easy, then everybody would be doing it. So, yes, change is essential to improving your business, and your will to change is what will set you apart from your competition.

Before you can change your business, you must first take an honest look at where your business is today and where *you* currently are as the leader of your business. One of the most famous lines from William Shakespeare's *Hamlet* is, "To thine own self be true."

To improve yourself and your business, you must be not only willing but eager to confront brutal truths. Only through a fully truthful look at yourself and your business will you be able to enact the changes needed to make you and your business the very best they can be. Here are some examples of what I feel are my own personal strengths and weaknesses.

One of my biggest strengths is the ability to focus on the immediate task at hand while at the same time juggling multiple projects during each day. Another of my strengths is the ability to motivate large groups of people to rally behind a common goal.

On the flip side, one of my weaknesses is that I often believe in people more than they believe in themselves, assuming they will do exactly what they say they will do. Ronald Reagan once said we needed to "trust but verify." I'm pretty good at the trust part but lousy at verification.

I also hate the numbers part of business. I like spending money—a lot. In fact, I honestly tell people that the reason I work so hard to make money is because I really love to spend money on myself and my family, to help my associates and their families, and to feel the joy of donating to charities I believe in. But the truth is, I don't enjoy the counting and accounting part of business. Once I finally realized this weakness, I was able to turn over the accounting part of our company to a firm that does love to handle these details and truly excels at it.

You need to do a similar exercise and identify your personal strengths and weaknesses as the leader of your business. After that, it's time to do the same for your business. Start by thinking of your business as if it were also a person—an individual with its own strengths and weaknesses.

Here are some examples from my businesses.

Dream Big!

One of our biggest strengths is *customization*. We refuse to accept one-size-fits-all. A company that wants to be all things to all people will end up being nothing to all people or all things to no people—and both of those are bad! Another reason I named my former company FishBait is that we "bait the hook to suit the fish and not the fisherman." Our fish are our customers, and we want them to know it's about them, not about us. That's the kind of customization with which we excel.

But one of our weaknesses is that the president of the company—that would be me—takes on far too many projects because he hates leaving *any* fish in the ocean. That often overstresses our team's ability to deliver real value to each of our clients.

Once you've identified both your personal strengths and weaknesses and your business's strengths and weaknesses, you then need to decide which strengths you wish to build on and which weaknesses you wish to fix. You have essentially two choices for how to address weaknesses. One, you can gain the skills to fix them yourself; or two, you can hire someone else to fix them for you.

Once you know where you are and where your business is today, it's time to identify where you want to go. The Bible says in Proverbs 29:18, "Where there is no vision, the people perish." Dreams are the incubators of business and of life itself. The logo of Steven Spielberg's company DreamWorks is a boy fishing off a crescent moon.

I live in South Carolina, where our state's logo is the palmetto palm and the crescent moon. But personally, I prefer the full moon and full dreams. So, let's start with your *wildest* dreams.

Write Your Eulogy

Try this exercise. Close your eyes and imagine you are attending a funeral. The beautiful church is packed with flowers everywhere. All your friends and family are there. Can you see it? Oh yeah, I forgot to mention that it's *your* funeral. The clock has run out, I'm afraid.

Someone gets up to give your eulogy. In one sentence, what do you want them to say about you and your life? What will they say about what you did with your life? Do you like what they'll say, or do we need to rewrite that script? What do you really want them to say? Here's what I hope someone will say about me:

> *Rick Jones was a good and honorable man who always pulled his own weight and found a way to support his family and lots of others throughout his life while enjoying all the blessings of this world.*

Some key phrases here are:

- *Good and honorable*—I want to be remembered as honest, kind, thoughtful, and Godly.
- *Pulled his own weight*—I want to be known as someone who had strong initiative, work habits, and capacity and who made his own way.
- *Support*—I want to be viewed as unselfish, giving, and a friend.
- *Enjoying*—I want my family and friends to have enjoyed spending time with me as we did activities, sports, and trips and experienced food.

Think about what you want *your* personal vision to be. Now, let's do the same for your business. What do you want people to say? Here's an example of the vision for one of my businesses:

> *The vision of* The Business Tithe *is to help small businesses become more successful and profitable so that they can contribute more to helping their communities, while making a fair profit for our business at the same time and potentially leaving a long-lasting legacy.*

The vision for your business serves as a compass, always keeping you heading in the right direction. The true purpose of any business is to

The vision for your business serves as a compass, always keeping you heading in the right direction.

provide value to customers. So, once you have identified the vision for both yourself and your business, which I call the internal focus, it's time to look at your business from an external perspective.

I own a business called Heartland Pirates, which has five different verticals. One of these verticals writes, promotes, and distributes a variety of books. One vertical writes, produces, hosts, and distributes a podcast called *Sh-Boom*, aimed at baby boomers. One creates workshops and speaking engagements to help small businesses and assist aging baby boomers in finishing their lives strong and leaving a legacy. One is a sponsorship consultancy and sales representation vertical, and finally, one is a content production division that creates features such as the *United Tastes of America* series.

What's the common denominator? All are about storytelling because at my core, I am a storyteller. Here is the purpose of Heartland Pirates:

> *Heartland Pirates provides meaningful and measurable value to niche brands and businesses by reaching consumers in heartland states or consumers in all states who love traditional American values, and doing so in a fun, swashbuckling style reflective of pirates of yore.*

Our tagline is "Navigating consumers and brands to new lands." We are serious about our work but don't take ourselves too seriously. So, what is the purpose of your business? Why does your business exist? Whom do you serve? And how do you serve?

Know Your Why, Whom, and How

The *why* is critical because it must be something wanted and needed in the marketplace. The *whom* is your precise customer base. The *how* is what you offer that is different from what similar companies offer to the same customers to meet the same needs. These are not only your products and services but also the ways in which you offer and deliver these products and services.

Let's start with the external question of *why*. What is the market need for your business? The *why* for Heartland Pirates is pretty simple. The marketing and communications world in America is largely coastally biased and fails to understand consumers from flyover states or those who value traditional American ideals, such as community, faith, family, patriotism, and respect for institutions and traditions. We reach those underserved consumers in a variety of ways, always seeking to provide value for their lifestyles and for their values and principles.

Next, let's identify your customers. It's been said that *riches are in the niches*. You must commit to serving the right customers. Each of my previous three agencies, while sharing the corporate sponsorship marketing space, had entirely different target customers.

The first agency, The Strategic Group, evolved from Rick Jones & Associates to Strategic Sports Specialists. We grew from a locally relevant firm to a nationally recognized agency. We created and implemented trade and consumer marketing activation programs by focusing on consumer food product manufacturers such as Nabisco, Kraft, and Frito-Lay and leading grocery chains such as Kroger, Raley's, Bruno's, and H-E-B, to whom we sold title sponsorships to community-oriented sporting events such as PGA TOUR golf tournaments. Our unique specialty grew out of our understanding of both grocery retailers and food manufacturers.

My second agency, The GEM Group, focused on activating sponsorship programs for Fortune 100 companies that sponsored large-scale sports and entertainment events, including the Olympic Games,

FIFA Soccer World Cups, and NCAA basketball tournaments. These clients included Sears, Bank of America, UPS, and Coca-Cola, among others. This agency gained global recognition as we activated programs worldwide.

My third agency, FishBait Marketing (later FishBait Solutions), focused largely on college sports. We represented college football and basketball coaches' trade associations and sold corporate sponsorships to companies that wanted to use highly recognizable coaches in their marketing programs. We also sold assets from both special events run by the coaches' trade organizations and the charities supported by the coaches' organizations. And our customers included both these entities within college sports and the corporations that marketed their products and services to college sports fans.

As you can see, while similar, each of these businesses had different and very specific customer targets. To be successful, you must think about your ideal customers or customer segments. What are the demographics and psychographics of your current and prospective customers?

For those of you who sell products or services to other businesses, this is where I remind you that I have never seen a *business* buy anything. It's *human beings* who do the buying. So, let's look at similarities and differences in the actual people you sell to. What are their ages, genders, nationalities, education levels, hobbies, etc.?

An *affinity group* is loosely defined as a collection of people with common interests. But one of my mentors, Chuck Jarvie, describes an affinity group as "a group of people who will suspend rational behavior in order to pursue their passions." I love that definition. Those are the types of customers you really desire because they are usually price insensitive. They are fans of yours and see great value in your products and services. That's why most successful businesses sell to *fans*; fans of their products, services, and staff members.

One thing I have seen is that businesses often forget about their loyal customers in the quest of trying to get new customers. This is a big mistake. You cannot abandon your base as you grow. To paraphrase singer-songwriter Stephen Stills, if you can't be with the one you love, *you'd better* love the one you're with.

Now, let's go even deeper with the analysis of your current customers. I'm a big proponent of the old 80/20 rule—the notion that 20 percent of your customers will contribute 80 percent of your profits. It's crucial to identify the 20 percent who are currently your best customers and to make some connections as to why they specifically value your business.

Is it the products and services you sell to them? Is it the price or the value of these products and services? Is it based on other things, such as convenience, service, quality guarantees, money-back offers, or something else? Or is it simply the way you and your team make your customers feel?

Define Your Goals

Understanding your customer is critical to the ultimate success of your business. Now that you have identified the strengths and weaknesses of your business, along with your vision for and purpose of your business, it's time to define exactly what *success* looks like for your business.

When I was a first-year teacher and head basketball coach at Frederica Academy in 1976, I received a book from one of my students about Coach Bobby Knight. You might remember that the 1976 Indiana Hoosiers, coached by Bobby Knight, remain to this day

Understanding your customer is critical to the ultimate success of your business.

the last team to go undefeated in a college basketball season. In his book, Coach Knight articulated the best definition of success I had ever seen or have seen since. He said, "Success is performing to the limits of your potential."[5] I love that definition, as it highlights that you're only limited by yourself, not by others.

So, what is *your* definition of personal success, and how does your business facilitate that success? And once you've figured that out, how do you define success for your business? Answering these questions provides context for what you need to do next to make your business as high performing as it can be.

At this point in your business analysis, you may realize that what your business needs is a total reinvention. There's an old saying that you can't teach an old dog new tricks. Well, it's a good thing you're not a dog. Sometimes, situations change to the point where only drastic measures will do. And at times, these are external changes that are totally out of your control.

SOMETIMES, YOU NEED TO REINVENT YOURSELF

History is full of stories of business reinvention. One example is Hermès, a French company that originally made and sold horse harness products and accessories. So, what do you do when the majority of people quit using horses for transportation? You take the skills you had before to produce other leather goods, such as belts and handbags, and ultimately, to produce scarves and other fashion items.

In 1993, our agency was fortunate to win the Sara Lee Knit Products Olympic Games sponsorship activation business. Sara Lee Knit Products, at that time, included such brands as Champion,

---

5 Bob Knight and Bob Hammel, *The Power of Negative Thinking: An Unconventional Approach to Achieving Positive Results* (New Harvest, 2013).

Hanes, and Playtex, but by far the most profitable division of the Sara Lee Knit Products was the L'eggs hosiery division.

In 1994, L'eggs was the title sponsor of the US Figure Skating Olympic trials. You might remember it as the event where Tonya Harding's ex-husband attacked Nancy Kerrigan. What I remember is that during that era, *everywhere* you looked, you found the famous pantyhose brand packaged in a plastic egg carton. The brand was heavily advertised, readily available via multiple retailers, and priced fairly.

Today, you rarely see L'eggs anywhere. What happened? Simply put, women quit wearing pantyhose. Today, women often opt for pants or casual skirts without stockings. No matter how good, available, or fairly priced a product is, it is not going to be successful if people don't want to use it. You can't control that. You can only adapt to it, and Sara Lee failed to read the tea leaves and innovate by producing products women wanted—such as leggings. However, there is now a renewed popularity. Fashion is cyclical, but maybe it is not too late for L'eggs.

This reminds me of a story of a dog food manufacturer whose new and improved product was failing miserably in the marketplace. The VP of marketing called his sales team to an emergency meeting. In that meeting, he pointed out that they had the most nutritious product on the market, the best packaging, terrific point-of-sale materials, national distribution, and award-winning advertising.

So, he asked, "What's the problem?" No one in the room said anything, so he repeated his question, louder this time. Finally, a voice came from the back of the room: "The dogs won't eat it." If you have a product that "dogs won't eat," it's time for reinvention.

The business world is constantly buffeted by external changes—general economic shifts, new technology replacing old processes, new inventions replacing old ones, and key accounts moving to competitors. Sometimes, you must contend with internal changes, such as the loss of a key associate or personal issues affecting you, the owner. Whatever the reason, there may come a point at which you realize you must totally change the nature of your business.

Does your business need a subtle tweak or a radical reinvention? Only you can determine that. By now, you should have done three significant things: identified and articulated the *vision* for your business, identified and articulated the *purpose* of your business, and identified and articulated the current *strengths and weaknesses* of both your business and yourself personally. Now, the fun part begins. It's time to set goals, so let's start with a little fun.

SET PERSONAL GOALS

You've heard of the bucket list, those things you want to do in your life before you kick the bucket. Do you have such a list? I have a *long* list of things I still want to do in my life and in my business career, including dishes I want to cook and eat, places where I want to travel, and new things I want to learn and experience. I even hope to write both a novel and a Broadway musical. I review my bucket list annually to decide which items I want to check off in the coming year.

Leisure travel is very important to me. I've been to each of the fifty states and to forty-one different countries. I have a *long* list of places I still want to go to; in fact, I have a detailed plan for where I want to go and when for the next ten years, God willing.

I now have three grandsons, and I have a list of places I want to take them and things I want to do with them both individually and together. I'm also intentional each year in writing down projects I want to do at my home and in my garden, new places where I want to eat, and things I want to learn to cook. I'm not only a planner but a *squeezer*, someone who squeezes out all life has to offer. And you know what? It seems the more things I write down that I want to do, the more things I actually get done.

As I previously said, I like making money because I *really* like spending money—on lots of things that please me, my family, and my friends—and having the resources to help others. So try adding helping others to your list, and you'll begin to see how many people you are able to help. Sit down sometime soon and make up your own bucket list.

SET BUSINESS GOALS

Now, let's jump into goals for your business. First, let's start at the finish line. I know that sounds like a backward plan, but then again, that's the point. Once you know where you want to end up, it's a whole lot easier to start making the plan to get you there.

What's your plan for your business after you've gone? Do you want to sell it? Leave it to a family member? Leave it for someone else on your team? Merge it with another entity? Or maybe just close the doors and ride off into the sunset? For you baby boomers, that sunset may be a lot closer than you think. Over the next twenty years, we will have the largest wealth transfer in the history of the world. Part of that transfer may be what you plan to do with your business.

There's no right or wrong answer, just *your* answer. And, of course, you may change your mind or direction over the course of your business life because there may be unanticipated changes in your life and in your business. But right now, what is your vision for your business at the finish line?

OK, now let's move from the end back to *today*. No matter what day or month it is in the year, let's begin with your annual goals. Each December, I sit down and reflect on the successes and accomplishments of the past year and also make a list of things we wanted to accomplish that did not happen as we'd planned. Then, I start listing my goals for the upcoming year. I am very intentional in what I feel we can accomplish each year, and I write down all of our goals, no matter how small.

We start with our financial goals. We must plan to make a profit in order to meet our expense obligations. We also need to plan for managing our cash flow as part of achieving our financial goals.

Part of our goals is retention-based—current business lines, products, and customers we intend to keep. Part of our goals are *new* products or lines of business we intend to launch, new customers we intend to pursue, and new expertise we intend to acquire. We have goals for top-line growth, bottom-line profitability, and market share gains. We have goals for current and new staff training and promotions. We have established goals for our marketing and communications efforts. And we have goals for annual meetings, planning retreats, and celebrations! All are important.

We also do scenario planning. If *this* happens, then we'll do *that*, such as adding staff or equipment or making personnel cuts or other budget-reducing activities.

Several years ago, I started a retirement program called a SEP, with tax-deferred dollars put into each of my associates' retirement accounts. We did this to give them a head start on retirement funds. But once the coronavirus came around, our business completely stopped, and we had zero income. Thankfully, we had these SEP funds available for each of our associates to use. It reminds me of the Bible story in which Joseph persuaded the pharaoh of Egypt to store up grain in the good times before the drought years came. Well, I had not intended on any drought years, but we were fortunately ready when they came. And—I finally learned the hard way—they always come.

If you want specific outcomes, you'll need to develop *specific* goals for all phases of your business. Annual goals are like a road map. They show all the places you want to go and how to get there. But many things can change, and that's why you must break down your annual goals into pieces.

First, you break them down into quarterly goals. I like to do this one month before the quarter begins, but you can start this at any time during the year. Then, I set monthly goals, followed by weekly goals and, ultimately, daily goals.

It's important to list daily goals *before* you develop your daily to-do list to make sure you are doing the right things to move your business along.

I also write down my *reward* for the day daily. My old boss at Georgia Tech, the late and great Dr. Homer Rice, got me into this habit. Each day, I select one thing I will do for myself—or for someone else—that serves as my reward for the day. It could be a phone call to an old friend, a walk with my dog, cooking a special meal, watching a sporting event, or a movie night with my wife. At the end of the year, I can look back and see 365 rewards. After all, *life* is why we work, and reviewing all those daily rewards keeps us both balanced and motivated.

Once you have created and, most importantly, written down all your annual, quarterly, monthly, weekly, and daily goals, let's take a few minutes to go deeper into specific elements of these goals. It all starts with finances. There are four key components to financial planning: income, cash flow, expenses, and profits.

Specific income goals are key. The ability to predict exactly what, where, and when you will gain income is crucial to running a successful small business. Our annual financial goals start with income sources and what we need to do to grow our income.

The second critical element is cash flow. For small businesses, cash is king. You can't pay your bills if you don't have the money in the bank. Our business demands that we project cash flow on a monthly basis. Your business might be different; you might have to project it on a weekly or even a daily basis. Like most small businesses, we occasionally need to borrow money, either from our own savings or through a bank loan, to cover our costs. Our projections allow us to predict when this might occur and make plans accordingly.

Third, you must predict annual expenses. We create an annual expense projection budget, which we then break down into monthly expense projections. Some things, such as payroll, health insurance, and business insurance, are easy to predict, while others are more difficult. Computer hard drives crash, printers break, meetings get rescheduled or canceled after you've purchased air tickets, and clients stick you with a huge restaurant bill or ask you for a donation to *their* favorite charity. Plus, sometimes you get a new project that requires you to pay for expenses up front before the client pays you.

We are now in the content creation business, producing everything from music videos to television commercials and more. We must manage film shoot budgets, which include expenses such as travel, actors' fees, catering, and site fees. This is yet a new level of financial complexity.

But the fact is, you cannot spend any more than you make, and expense projections help you make good decisions about unexpected costs and financial issues. If you do overspend, then there won't be any profits. So, every business should project its profit margins and actual profits.

Too often, I find that small businesses don't factor profits into their business plans, and guess what? They wind up with no profits. As I stated before, at Heartland Pirates, as at each of our other previous companies, we seek a 20 percent profit on gross income for the year. Not every project produces a 20 percent margin, but our annual goal is 20 percent from the collective income. Sometimes, we will take a smaller margin in order to win a new customer or start a new business venture, but we will *never*—and I mean *never*—undertake any project without *some* profit baked in. Nor should you.

SET PERSONNEL GOALS

Now onto the next stage of goal setting. There are only two ways that I know of to make the team at your business more successful: Make your players better or get better players. The truth is that most small businesses must do both.

You will need to sit with each of your associates and develop their goals. Their individual goals should follow the same formula (annual, monthly, weekly, etc.) you've already used for your business. Establishing measurable goals for each of your people will enable you to maximize their strengths and improve their weaknesses. Personnel goals allow you to project when it's time to promote someone. They will also tell you when it might be time to replace someone—and what exact skills were lacking in that associate that you'll need to find in their replacement.

Developing personnel goals is time-intensive but incredibly valuable. A business should run like a rowing crew team, with all the oars going in the same direction at the same time. Individual goals juxtaposed against the overall business goals keep those disparate oars moving in the right direction.

At Heartland Pirates, we're also big on articulating specific goals for each of our customers, prospects, and projects, each and every year. We start with all our current clients and make some judgments about retaining the same level of billings or what we need to do in order to grow revenues. We also project where we might have less revenue for a variety of reasons, such as having to pay a third-party supplier to provide a service that we don't offer.

We then develop very specific annual plans for each existing customer, with aspects such as changes from the previous year, how to balance retaining both the business and the billings, how to grow billings, what is new to offer, how else we can help our client, and how to staff the business based on new information.

After planning for our existing clients, we turn our attention to who we feel are our best prospects to become new customers for us. We are very intentional in our specific goals for prospects. How many new clients can we realistically handle? What part of the year do we have excess capacity? What *types* of prospects do we want? Determining the kind of customers or prospects you want to attract is significant and important. As I've said earlier, there are riches in the niches. I enjoy identifying highly targeted prospects, and each year, we set a goal to close a predetermined number of these.

Goals are your road map for your business, but remember that a road map is only as good as your automobile, the roads you'll drive on, the availability of gasoline, and the skills of the driver.

That leads to step five—planning and execution. Because this is the part where the rubber meets the road—the part that allows you to produce the profit that you will share with your flocks.

Goals are your road map for your business, but remember that a road map is only as good as your automobile, the roads you'll drive on, the availability of gasoline, and the skills of the driver.

Whatever you do, work at it with all your heart.

—COLOSSIANS 3:23

STEP FIVE

PLAN AND EXECUTE

ULTIMATELY, WHAT SEPARATES an exceptional business from a less-than-fully successful business is planning and execution. If goals are the *talk*, then plans are the *walk*, and to be successful, you must *walk the talk*. Plans are the specific steps you are going to take to make all your goals come to fruition.

For every business goal you've outlined, you will now need a plan to make that goal come true. Planning rolls out in four stages:

- Stage #1: List each task required to accomplish the goal.
- Stage #2: Determine the resources required to reach the goal.
- Stage #3: List the potential obstacles you may need to overcome to reach the goal.
- Stage #4: Identify the timelines required to reach the goal.

Let's begin with the list of tasks required for each goal. To do this, let me share a couple of examples, starting with an especially difficult one.

Experiencing a Heart Attack

In October 2023, I had a heart attack and had a stent put in where I had a blockage. My cardiologist said I needed to lose twenty-five pounds. He felt that the extra weight I was carrying was not good for my health, and it also did not align with the physical image I wanted people to see. Some people eat to live, while I live to eat, so I knew I needed to make some changes. So, what were the specific tasks I needed to plan to reach this goal?

First, I had to change my diet. When I eat carbs, I not only don't lose weight but also tend to gain even more. So, I created a specific diet that limits carbohydrate intake. I didn't say I'd eliminate carbs completely, because that would be unreasonable for me. I allow myself two days a week to enjoy some of my favorite carbs, such as pasta and biscuits. I tend to lose weight when I eat more fresh vegetables; plenty of dairy products, such as cheese; and healthy proteins, such as lean meats, seafood, and eggs. So, diet was a major part of my plan.

Second, I needed to increase the amount of exercise I was doing. I have bad knees from previous meniscus surgeries and one knee replacement and cannot run long distances to lose weight, so my plans included three elements: *long* daily walks of at least four miles each day; workouts at a gym or swimming in my pool at least four times per week; and lots of yard work, including planting, raking, weeding, and other activities.

This combination of a specific diet and exercise plan, with proper metrics to track my progress, created the perfect plan for me to meet the goal of losing twenty-five pounds.

Achieving a Specific Business Goal

A second example is a plan to achieve a specific *business* goal. One of my former clients is the Atlantic Coast Conference (ACC). The ACC is one of the premier collegiate athletic conferences in the country, comprising eighteen schools across twelve states, with the majority of schools located on the Eastern Seaboard.

Our job was to find corporate sponsors that would leverage the assets of the conference to build value for both the sponsor and our client. In order to produce value for both entities, we also had to produce value for the fans of the ACC schools. Corporate sponsorship works best when both the conference and the sponsor jointly bring value to themselves by bringing real value to ACC fans.

The ACC was, at the time, at somewhat of a competitive disadvantage from some other conferences, such as the SEC, Big Ten, and

Big 12, because it did not have a dedicated television network. (Note: It does now, as the ACC Network started in the fall of 2019.) Each of those conferences with TV networks has one or more shows that originate from its respective schools.

This allows fans of those schools and their conferences to see the conference in aggregation and develops pride among its fans. To promote the coming of the new network, we developed a tour for the ACC to go to each campus. One of our major business goals for the ACC in 2016 was to secure an underwriting presenting sponsor for our ACC Football Tailgate Tour to travel to each of our schools during the football season.

The planning we go through to sell sponsorships includes a process we call *architecture and engineering*. Architecture involves developing tour elements and identifying saleable and leverageable activities for sponsors. Engineering is the matching of those assets and elements with appropriate sponsor prospects.

A big part of the architectural planning process is finding or creating activities that fans want to see and do. We wanted the fans of ACC Football to be excited about the tour and the upcoming network and to spend some of their game-day time with us. One way is to have legendary players make appearances, sign autographs, and pose for photos with fans. We used this idea as bait to secure our tour's initial presenting sponsor, Lumber Liquidators.

We also explored other relevant activities for a pregame tailgate-themed tour, including food-related activities and children's activities, such as face painting and music. The second part of planning is determining the resources needed to fulfill the goal. These include what kinds of staff skills will be needed, what additional personnel would be required, and what financial costs would be incurred.

DIFFERENT STRATEGIES ARE NEEDED

With each challenge, I needed a different strategy. For my weight-loss program plan, I needed to purchase both a Fitbit to measure how far I travel each day and how many calories I burn and a scale to see how many pounds I had lost. I also needed to determine and schedule the proper amount of time for physical activities.

For the ACC Football Tailgate Tour, we needed lots of research on sponsor prospects to prepare compelling sales presentations. We also had to budget an appropriate amount of money for travel expenses to visit and present to those prospects. And we had to produce multimedia presentations and collateral materials to showcase the opportunity and capture the excitement.

The third part of planning involves identifying the obstacles you will need to overcome to achieve your goal. For my weight loss plan, most of the obstacles are mental, such as how to stay away from tempting foods. How do I put in the necessary exercise and physical activity time, given the significant amount of travel in my schedule? How can I stay mentally strong and committed to the goal?

One way was to post my goal on my bathroom mirror, so I saw it first thing in the morning and last thing at night. As I traveled, I took bags of nuts with me to nibble on throughout the day to prevent food cravings, and I made sure I had my workout clothes with me on every trip.

For selling sponsorships for the ACC Tour, the biggest obstacle is handling rejection. When you really believe you have the perfect opportunity for a business or brand and your thinking is rejected, no matter the reason, it hurts and can be discouraging. The answer is grinding and making the needed extra calls every day to ultimately make the sale.

The final piece of the planning puzzle is creating appropriate timelines. After all, goals are deliverables with deadlines. Timelines allow you to monitor where you are on the journey to reach the goal.

For my weight loss plan, I set a mini goal of losing one pound per week, which would enable me to reach my goal in six months. I also thought that a gradual and consistent weight loss program would produce more lasting results, that is, keeping the weight off once I'd lost it. I monitor my Fitbit daily, but I only weigh myself once a week, on Friday mornings. If I have reached my weight goal on Friday, then I might celebrate with a little food over the weekend. And if I have failed, I can use the weekend for extra exercise.

When you are selling an event such as a tour, you must monitor progress because the tour has to happen at a specific time. For the football tour, I knew we would need to have a presenting sponsor on board before the ACC Football media days in mid-July.

But a not-so-funny thing happened on the way to the forum. We failed to sell the 2017 ACC Tailgate Tour because our title sponsor, Lumber Liquidators, went through hard times and did not renew. Welcome to real life in the business world. Despite all our plans, we failed to get a sponsor needed to make the tour a reality. It wasn't for lack of trying, but you don't win by trying. That's why it's so important not to put all your eggs in any one basket. Because eggs break, and sometimes, business initiatives don't work out.

EXECUTION IS CRITICAL

Coach John Wooden once said, "By failing to prepare, you are preparing to fail." Plans are your preparation instructions. Every business is different, so you now need to look at your specific goals and outline your plans accordingly. After completing your plans, now comes the time to do what Nike's slogan says and "Just do it." In other words, execute your plan.

I previously told you that I am a big dreamer, a consummate planner, and a life squeezer. I am also a grinder. A grinder is someone who does whatever it takes to execute their plans. Execution requires discipline, perseverance, and borderline obsession.

In the previous chapters, I've outlined a planning strategy, but as the wise man once said, you can lead a horse to water, but you can't make it drink. All the planning in the world results in nothing if the plan never gets executed. I can *show* you how to run a profitable and meaningful business successfully, but neither I nor anyone else can make you do it. Only you, the business owner, can execute your plan.

I love to cook and spend a lot of time in my kitchen. Talk about execution—cooking may be the *ultimate* execution task. You can have five-star recipes, fresh organic ingredients, and expensive cooking utensils, but it all comes down to how you use them—how you execute.

For my various businesses, execution starts with my daily to-do list. The weekend before each week, I outline my weekly to-dos by day; then, I rewrite my daily list in specific half-hour increments the night before. I also maintain an annual calendar with key events, meetings, and activities, which I refer to daily. Importantly, my to-do list comes directly from my written business plans, enabling me to prioritize activities and maximize my outputs.

Our operational activities align with the needs of both our clients and the marketplace. We find that there is a certain rhythm to our business, with specific deliverables on certain days of the week. Therefore, we plan our weekly activities based on a variety of external elements.

We hold our weekly staff meetings early on Monday mornings to identify each person's tasks for the week and ensure all our prioritized activities are completed on time. We also speak with all our major clients each Monday to share what we plan to do for them that week and to highlight upcoming events. This helps our clients see that we have a clear plan for them every week.

We rarely, if ever, try to *sell* anything on a Monday. I laughingly say that all God's children hate Mondays. So, we try not to pitch anything new on a day when people are not necessarily in their most cheerful and expansive mind frame. Conversely, all God's children love Fridays, so we *love* selling at the end of the week.

I try to make my weekly schedule consistent. On Mondays, I lead the staff meeting and participate in all client calls. On Tuesdays, I work on projects and sales proposals. On Wednesdays, I write, update social media, record my podcast, and work on long-term planning. I try to be out in the marketplace or on Zoom making sales calls on Thursdays and Fridays. We often sell sophisticated and complex marketing programs, and I prefer presenting late in the week so the prospect can consider my proposal over the weekend.

You must, of course, build in time for the unexpected and know which things can wait until later. In running a business, there will always be interruptions and fires to put out—whether it's a staff member dealing with unplanned family issues or a client weathering an unexpected crisis. Or a major unexpected pandemic, such as the coronavirus, that creates unique problems due to no fault of your own.

Or perhaps there's no problem at all but rather some unique and timely new *opportunity* that deserves immediate attention. Another major time killer is unexpected and unscheduled telephone calls. I try to schedule all my daily calls in advance.

When I do get that unexpected call, I often let them leave a message first, then listen to see if it needs my immediate attention. I also tell people that I will call them at unique times, like 10:38 a.m., so they will remember and realize that I truly am busy. Additionally, I utilize a variety of time and project management tools, such as Microsoft Outlook and various smartphone apps, to stay on schedule and prevent me from dropping the ball.

BE CONSISTENT AND FLEXIBLE

However, the real key to my executive success is simply sticking to that to-do list. At the end of the day, execution is all about predetermined results. You should never be surprised when things work out favorably, only when they do not. You've planned in advance for success, and therefore, success should never be a surprise to you or anyone else on your team.

Flexibility is important, but productivity is *most* important. Remember to avoid confusing activity with achievement. The fact that you're busy does not make your busyness effective. As a business owner, you must make sure that each and every activity gets you closer to achieving your goals.

A big part of this is knowing what and when to delegate. A business owner needs to do just the things that only they can do and leave the rest to their teammates. Your detailed plans should help you make those delegation decisions. Nothing is a bigger time killer than jumping in to solve every single problem as it occurs. As the old country song says, "You've got to know when to hold them and know when to fold them." Sometimes you need to walk away and let your staff members do their jobs. Or better yet, *run* away, and *really* let your staff do their jobs.

But, finally, let's talk about accountability. You, the business owner, can assign both tasks and responsibility but *never* accountability. The buck always stops with the business owner. *Period.* It is up to you to closely monitor the way your associates execute the work to ensure they are accomplishing their goals in a timely manner.

At the end of the day, business is all about *planning your work and working your plan*. Execution is nothing more or less than implementing your plan daily.

Pray then in this way …
Thy kingdom come;
Thy will be done,
on earth as it is in heaven.

—MATTHEW 5:9–10

STEP SIX

PRAY FOR SUCCESS

IN THE LORD'S Prayer, Jesus prays to his Father, "Thy will be done, on earth as it is in heaven." We are God's hands on earth. For God's will to be done on earth, we must work. But first, we need to connect to that higher purpose.

Step six is to pray for the success of your business in a very intentional way.

My former business partner, Ron Cook, has a wonderful way of starting every day. He calls it *thanking* and *thinking*. He first writes down everything he is thankful for from the previous day. It's kind of hard to stay in a bad mood once you acknowledge all the very real blessings in your life—gifts such as your family; your friends; your church, synagogue, or mosque; your business; your business associates; vendors; and customers, as well as your home, city, country, and that great big, wonderful world at-large.

Ron then shifts to the thinking part, listing everything he needs and wants to accomplish that day. He then prays specifically and intentionally for these things to happen. Finally, he goes about doing everything within his power, using all his abilities and best efforts, to make those things happen. Ron has encouraged me to follow his lead, and since I have started doing this, my business—and my life—has been blessed even beyond my wildest dreams and expectations. I consider it essential for you to pray daily for the success of your business and for the success of your family, your associates, your customers and vendors, your community and country, and the world at-large.

God wants your business to succeed to feed his sheep, and he answers prayers. Jesus guaranteed this when he said, "Ask, and it will be given to you; seek, and you will find; knock, and it will be opened to you" (Matthew 7:6). Don't let a day begin without finding that door and knocking.

Prayer is both an act of humility and an act of boldness.

When you pray for the success of your business, you are not simply asking God to bless your bottom line. You are aligning your heart with his purposes and placing your work under his authority. Prayer is both an act of humility and an act of boldness. It reminds you that every talent, opportunity, and connection you have is a gift from God, while also giving you courage to ask him to multiply those gifts for his glory.

Praying for success should also move beyond self-interest. When you ask God to prosper your business, include in that prayer the well-being of your employees, customers, vendors, and community. Ask that your work might create value that blesses others, provides livelihoods, and contributes to the common good. Business can be a powerful platform for ministry, and prayer helps you keep that perspective front and center.

Praying "Thy will be done" is a statement of confidence that God's plans are greater than ours. Sometimes, success looks like growth and expansion. Other times, it comes in the form of pruning and redirection. By praying with open hands, you invite God to shape your business into what he knows will bear the most fruit. In doing so, you discover that true success is not only in what you build but in who you become through the process.

For where your treasure is,
there your heart will be also.

—LUKE 12:34

STEP SEVEN

TITHE 10 PERCENT

AS MENTIONED EARLIER, I have a simple way of determining a person's priorities and what they really stand for by just looking at their checkbook.

When God created the earth, he worked for six days and rested on the seventh. He rested and admired his work, celebrating what he had accomplished. The noblest and best way for you to celebrate the success of your business and your life is to give a portion of your profits away. Christians call this tithing, and the Bible says that God asks each person to give back 10 percent to him. I hope each of you already personally tithe by giving at least 10 percent of the income you take home from your business to your place of worship.

But what if we went one step further, and each small business contributed an *additional* 10 percent of its post-tax profits annually to a cause you and your people—your associates, customers, suppliers—really cared about. I would never specifically suggest what that cause or charity should be, for only you and your people know in your hearts what you'd like to support. It could be food for those who have little, housing for those without, or shelters for women and children in need. It could be cancer research or Little League Baseball or a local art museum, or everything in between and beyond.

Business owners must find time to count their blessings and to share these blessings with others in order to change and improve the world. There is no reason why anyone in America should go to bed hungry, not be able to afford their medications, or not have a roof over their head each night. We are so blessed that we should be able to share our resources and take care of all of our people.

Think about it. What if all small businesses in this nation took just 10 percent of their business profits and did something beneficial for their local communities and society at-large with that money? My guess is that we'd never have to ask the government to fund anything except, perhaps, infrastructure, national defense, and governmental operating costs.

At our companies, we have supported many different charities, but we especially care about children's charities. Locally, we now support Epworth Children's Home, a safe and caring place for children whose parents are homeless or displaced for various reasons, such as drug addiction or incarceration. Nationwide, we support Covenant House, a special organization in New York City and other locations that helps runaway teenagers. Internationally, we send support to Sylvia's Children—a charity started by my dear friend and small business owner Sylvia Allen—which funds an orphanage in Uganda and cares for hundreds of children in that country.

We also support Samaritan's Feet, a charity that provides shoes for those in need. Sometimes, we feel called to help others immediately. In December 2021, massive, destructive tornadoes struck eleven counties in western Kentucky, causing great damage. We were able to use our business tithe to quickly send money to The Governor's Fund for the people affected in those counties.

What if all small businesses did what a lot of large companies do and allowed their associates time off for community service?

I was raised a good Southern Baptist, but I married an even better Methodist and have been a Methodist for the past forty years. The Reverend John Wesley, founder of the Methodist Church, told his parishioners, "Do all the good you can. By all the means you can. In all the ways you can. In all the places you can. At all the times you can. To all the people you can. As long as ever you can."

I encourage you to make the commitment to the business tithe and decide what you and your business would like to support. Sit with your team and start a conversation today about what your heart is telling you to support. And then, just do it!

If you're a baby boomer business owner who is looking for your exit strategy, I encourage you to include charity as part of that strategy. You will now have the chance to turn your success into significance. Significance is the legacy you and your business will leave behind.

As God admired what he had done on the seventh day, this final step, the business tithe, will allow you to know that you and your business are making and will continue to make a real difference to others in need.

So, there you have it.

Seven simple steps to make your business the best it can be and to provide resources to feed sheep in your community and throughout the world, not only for today but also for the future.

This is what God asks of us, and it's what America needs, now more than ever. And, in return, God will keep his promise to you, the business owner. As Jeremiah 29:11–12 says, "'For I know the plans I have for you,' declares the Lord, 'plans to prosper you and not to harm you, plans to give you hope and a future.'"

God bless you and yours each and every day.

If you're a baby boomer business owner who is looking for your exit strategy, I encourage you to include charity as part of that strategy. You will now have the chance to turn your success into significance. Significance is the legacy you and your business will leave behind.

CONCLUSION

If you found this book helpful, contact me directly for more resources and tools for improving your business. Or get in touch to schedule me for a speaking engagement.

My email address is rick@heartlandpirates.com, and my cell phone number is 843-412-5605.

I'd love to hear from you.

www.ingramcontent.com/pod-product-compliance
Lightning Source LLC
LaVergne TN
LVHW090617110826
845146LV00001B/421

* 9 7 9 8 8 9 1 8 8 3 8 6 4 *